Verbal Reasoning

10 Minute Tests

11⁺–12⁺ years

Test 1: Sorting Words 1

Underline the word in the brackets which goes best with the words given outside the brackets.

Example: word, paragraph, sentence (pen, cap, <u>letter</u>, top, stop)

1. chat, converse (read, gossip, lecture, preach, pray)
2. improvise, devise (invent, plan, prepare, train, examine)
3. succinct, concise (wordy, rambling, flawed, formal, precise)
4. scandal, shame (belief, honour, distance, disgrace, worship)
5. guard, shield (disregard, observe, notice, study, protect)

Underline the two words, one from each group, which are closest in meaning.

Example: (race, shop, <u>start</u>) (finish, <u>begin</u>, end)

6. (eager, indifferent, content) (enthusiastic, different, equal)
7. (tribute, celebration, crisis) (security, danger, dilemma)
8. (rush, charge, toss) (catch, entrust, turn)
9. (suffer, falter, perish) (control, master, die)
10. (tease, enrage, encourage) (infuriate, tickle, magnify)

Underline the word in the brackets closest in meaning to the word in capitals.

Example: UNHAPPY (unkind death laughter <u>sad</u> friendly)

11. STALE (fresh stark post stem mouldy)
12. ENVY (jealousy sympathy pity support understanding)
13. COARSE (refined polite fine smooth rough)
14. GYRATE (strike slide swirl count pounce)
15. ESTEEM (disrespect admire despise mock criticise)

Underline the pair of words most similar in meaning.

Example: come, go <u>roam, wander</u> fear, fare

16. wash, dry bubble, soap twitter, babble
17. glimmer, glitter tinsel, tree gloomy, cheerful
18. class, school type, category record, omission
19. sumptuous, luxurious dull, sharp wealthy, poor
20. consume, consider breakfast, dinner peckish, hungry

TEST 2: **Sorting Words 2**

Test time: 0 5 10 minutes

Underline the two words which are the odd ones out in the following groups of words.

Example: black   <u>king</u>   purple   green   <u>house</u>

1	lane	path	pedestrian	car	way
2	gash	gush	rip	pour	slash
3	consider	think	considerable	large	substantial
4	trait	gift	feature	present	characteristic
5	graceful	lithe	awkward	elegant	bulky

Underline the one word in the brackets which will go equally well with both the pairs of words outside the brackets.

Example: rush, attack   cost, fee   (price, hasten, strike, <u>charge</u>, money)

6	confident, courageous	strong, striking	(paint, brave, bold, modest, vivid)
7	conceal, suppress	envelop, cloak	(replace, cover, insure, include, travel)
8	portrait, likeness	concept, idea	(picture, illustration, plan, painting, image)
9	recline, rest	untruth, fib	(falsehood, prostrate, lounge, lie, evade)
10	school, teach	locomotive, engine	(motor, steam, learn, train, develop)

Find a word that is similar to the word in capital letters and that rhymes with the second word.

Example: CABLE   tyre   <u>wire</u>

11	ESCAPE	white	_____
12	FIRE	claim	_____
13	PURCHASED	caught	_____
14	ASCEND	rhyme	_____
15	DISBELIEVE	spout	_____

Underline one word in the brackets which is most opposite in meaning to the word in capitals.

Example: WIDE   (broad   vague   long   <u>narrow</u>   motorway)

16	LIGHT	(flimsy	delicate	gentle	insubstantial	heavy)
17	REMARKABLE	(ordinary	astonishing	extraordinary	striking	exceptional)
18	HINDER	(delay	help	hamper	obstruct	instruct)
19	PAST	(gift	present	failed	ended	overtaken)
20	REMOTE	(distant	near	far	isolated	remove)

Total

Test 3: Selecting Words 1

Underline two words, one from each group, that go together to form a new word. The word in the first group always comes first.

Example: (hand, <u>green</u>, for)   (light, <u>house</u>, sure)

1 (chop, walk, dressing) (chair, path, stick)
2 (cereal, hole, oat) (bowl, meal, wheat)
3 (side, out, drop) (down, law, low)
4 (building, high, black) (land, gear, spot)

Find a word that can be put in front of each of the following words to make new, compound words.

Example: CAST   FALL   WARD   POUR   __DOWN__

5 BONE   WARD   DATE   FIRE   _____
6 BULB   LIGHT   BACK   CARD   _____
7 PIPE   SCREEN WARD   SWEPT   _____
8 FLOWER SHINE   TAN   BURN   _____

Find the letter which will complete both pairs of words, ending the first word and starting the second. The same letter must be used for both sets of words.

Example: mea (t) able   fi (t) ub

9   smu (__) rain   stin (__) rown   11   roo (__) ake   fil (__) eat
10 fla (__) est   cul (__) ent   12   stri (__) elt   shrim (__) ear

Complete the following expressions by underlining the missing word.

Example: Frog is to tadpole as swan is to (duckling, baby, <u>cygnet</u>).

13 Comfort is to distress as favour is to (support, prefer, disapprove).
14 Measure is to weigh as divide is to (unite, distribute, combine).
15 Ruler is to millimeter as clock is to (time, minute, hands).
16 Familiar is to usual as original is to (novel, ordinary, copied).

Underline the pair of words most opposite in meaning.

Example: cup, mug   coffee, milk   <u>hot, cold</u>

17 spin, revolve   circle, ring   revolt, support
18 erect, upright   build, construct   assemble, dismantle
19 imperfect, flawless lacking, deficient   faulty, incomplete
20 benefit, handicap   advantage, asset   weakness, liability

TEST 4: **Selecting Words 2**

Test time: 0 5 10 minutes

Find the letter which will complete both pairs of words, ending the first word and starting the second. The same letter must be used for both sets of words.

Example: mea (t) able   fi (t) ub

1 bom (___) other   clim (___) reak
2 strang (___) ager   battl (___) mber
3 ironi (___) reak   mimi (___) aste
4 cal (___) leet   snif (___) rank

Find two letters which will end the first word and start the second word.

Example: rea (c h) air

5 tr (___ ___) rie   7 bea (___ ___) ips
6 ba (___ ___) ink   8 trif (___ ___) ather

Add one letter to the word in capital letters to make a new word. The meaning of the new word is given in the clue.

Example: PLAN simple ___PLAIN___

9   RAFT skill _____   11 SOON utensil _____
10 WEED cloth _____   12 TIED weary   _____

Move one letter from the first word and add it to the second word to make two new words.

Example: hunt sip   ___hut___   ___snip___

13 patient bran   _____ _____
14 wring   swam   _____ _____
15 parking night _____ _____
16 breathe spin   _____ _____

Change the first word into the last word, by changing one letter at a time and making two new, different words in the middle.

Example: TEAK ___TEAT___ ___TENT___ RENT

17 CROW _____ _____ LOOP
18 KNOB _____ _____ UNIT
19 SPIN _____ _____ SLUR
20 MAZE _____ _____ NICE

5

Total

TEST 5: Anagrams 1

Test time: 0　5　10 minutes

Rearrange the letters in capitals to make another word. The new word has something to do with the first two words.

Example:　spot, soil　　SAINT　__STAIN__

1　scanty, scarce　　SPARES　_____
2　eats, feasts　　SNIDE　_____
3　misery, dejection　　PRAISED　_____
4　chief, main　　PASTEL　_____
5　issue, provide　　PIQUE　_____
6　lift, hoist　　REVEL　_____

Find and underline the two words which need to change places for the sentence to make sense.

Example: She went to <u>letter</u> the <u>write</u>.

7　One can swim over she thousand metres.
8　Mixing green and yellow paint makes blue.
9　The room entered the children quietly and sat on the floor.
10　The sitting in the carpet room is too patterned.
11　It was raining outside hard.
12　Perhaps you can stay with I?

Look at the first group of three words. The word in the middle has been made from the other two words. Complete the second group of three words in the same way, making a new word in the middle.

Example:　PAIN　INTO　TOOK　　ALSO　__SOON__　ONLY

13	HIKE	KEEP	EPIC	MOST	_____	UNTO
14	BIRO	BIND	POND	TRAY	_____	FLIP
15	WORE	WINE	PINT	PORT	_____	CARS
16	READ	YEAR	YARD	GLUE	_____	BEEN
17	KIND	KILL	PULL	BOOK	_____	WITH
18	MAZE	SAME	MISS	TINY	_____	CAMP
19	TAKE	FLAT	FOOL	YARD	_____	BOAR
20	BUSH	WISH	WICK	PILE	_____	PONY

Total

TEST 6: Anagrams 2

Find the four-letter word hidden at the end of one word and the beginning of the next word. The order of the letters may not be changed.

Example: The children had bats and balls. ___sand___

1. Please remember to close the yellow door. _____
2. That old man is my grandfather. _____
3. Fragments of dinosaur bone are scattered there. _____
4. My teacher corrects our work every day. _____
5. The photographer's work is hung in this room. _____
6. You should lift the books carefully. _____
7. Seamus did not enjoy the party. _____
8. That bus arrives too soon for John to catch. _____

Find the three-letter word which can be added to the letters in capitals to make a new word. The new word will complete the sentence sensibly.

Example: The cat sprang onto the MO. ___USE___

9. The skater was able to GE along the ice with grace. _____
10. He ate up his carrots and CABE. _____
11. Kittens are extremely PFUL. _____
12. As the sun comes from behind the clouds, the sky LIGHS. _____
13. The ENTCE to the palace was very grand. _____
14. A THERMOER is an instrument for measuring temperature. _____

Find the four-letter word which can be added to the letters in capitals to make a new word. The new word will complete the sentence sensibly.

Example: At the zoo, we visited the REP house. ___TILE___

15. The students liked the teacher because he was very CING. _____
16. The ducklings were FOLLO their mother across the pond. _____
17. Someone who does not tell lies is HO. _____
18. The chef GD the carrot into slivers for the salad. _____
19. "Would Troy please RE to the school office." _____
20. At the class reunion people felt SENNTAL when the songs from their school days were played. _____

Test 7: Coded Sequences and Logic 1

A B C D E F G H I J K L M N O P Q R S T U V W X Y Z

Fill in the missing letters. The alphabet has been written out to help you.

Example: AB is to CD as PQ is to RS

1. TV is to QS as FH is to ____
2. QY is to RZ as SA is to ____
3. GH is to FI as ST is to ____
4. GD is to EB as CZ is to ____
5. DW is to EV as HS is to ____

A B C D E F G H I J K L M N O P Q R S T U V W X Y Z

Give the missing letters and numbers in the following sequences. The alphabet has been written out to help you.

Example: CQ DQ EP FP GO HO

6. RG ____ RE SD SC ____
7. aV dT ____ jP ____ pL
8. X3 Y4 Z5 ____ B7 ____
9. ____ 15T ____ 11S 9R 7R
10. XD ____ ZF ____ BH CI

Give the two missing numbers in the following sequences.

Example: 2 4 6 8 10

11. 2   3   ____ 8   12   ____
12. 2   ____ 8   ____ 32 64
13. 29 16 ____ 18 17   ____
14. ____ 21 ____ 31 36 41
15. 17 ____ 19 16 ____ 18

If a = 8, b = 6, c = 4, d = 3 and e = 2, find the value of the following calculations. Write your answer as a letter.

16. $\dfrac{ab}{c} - de$ = ____   19. $b^2 - ac$ = ____

17. $bd \div b$ = ____   20. $\dfrac{b^2}{d^2} \times e$ = ____

18. $(a + b + c) - cd$ = ____

8

TEST 8: Coded Sequences and Logic 2

A B C D E F G H I J K L M N O P Q R S T U V W X Y Z

Fill in the missing letters. The alphabet has been written out to help you.

Example: AB is to CD as PQ is to RS

1. UX is to VY as WZ is to ____
2. AZ is to CX as HS is to ____
3. HJ is to LN as RT is to ____
4. QM is to TP as UQ is to ____
5. HL is to GH as NR is to ____

A B C D E F G H I J K L M N O P Q R S T U V W X Y Z

Give the missing letters and numbers in the following sequences. The alphabet has been written out to help you.

Example: CQ DQ EP FP GO HO

#						
6	____	Z10	A15	B20	____	D30
7	PN	QO	____	____	TR	US
8	10I	____	12K	____	14M	15M
9	____	BY	CX	____	EV	FU
10	aJb	____	eNf	gPh	____	kTl

Give the two missing numbers in the following sequences.

Example: 2 4 6 8 10

#						
11	58	57	55	____	____	43
12	2	5	8	____	14	____
13	53	____	____	32	25	18
14	5	____	9	8	____	12
15	3	6	____	24	48	____

If p = 7, q = 3, r = 20, s = 5 and t = 15, find the value of the following calculations.

16. $2p - (q + s)$ = ____
17. $(r + s) \times (p - q)$ = ____
18. $s^2 + r + 2t$ = ____
19. $\dfrac{pr - (r + t)}{s}$ = ____
20. $\dfrac{qr}{s} + t$ = ____

TEST 9: Coded Sequences and Logic 3

Here are the codes for four words. Work out which code matches each word.

7 ^ 3 *	6 * ^ 3	7 * ^ 6	7 ^ 3 6
NEAR	BEAN	BARN	BARE

1 7 ^ 3 *   _____   3 7 * ^ 6   _____
2 6 * ^ 3   _____   4 7 ^ 3 6   _____

Using the same code, encode these words:

5 EARN   _____   6 ARENA   _____

Work out the following codes.

7   If the code for SQUARE is USWCTG, what is the code for DICED?   _____
8   If the code for POLICE is QPMJDF, what is the code for SPEED?   _____
9   If the code for LETTER is JCRRCP, what is the code for NOTES?   _____
10 If the code for WONDER is VNMCDQ, what is the code for SWISH?   _____

Pete has planted his vegetable garden in rows by his father's greenhouse. Using the information below, work out which vegetable is grown in each row.

| A |
| B |
| C |
| CARROTS |
| E |
| F |
| G |

GREENHOUSE

The lettuces and radishes are next to each other but neither is next to the carrots or the onions. The peas are next to the carrots. The herbs are closest to the greenhouse. The spinach is between the radishes and the carrots.

11–16   A = _____   D = CARROTS   G = _____
         B = _____   E = _____
         C = _____   F = _____

If November has five Sundays and the last Sunday is on the final day of the month, calculate the following:

17 What is the date of the first Sunday of the month?   _____
18 What day of the week is 3rd November?   _____
19 What date is the fourth Wednesday?   _____
20 Which other day of the week, beside Sunday, has five days in this November?   _____

10

TEST 10: Coded Sequences and Logic 4

Test time: 0 – 5 – 10 minutes

If G = 2, R = 6, O = 7, E = 4, T = 5 and S = 3, find the sum of the following words by adding their letters together.

1. OGRE _____
2. SORE _____
3. ROOT _____
4. TREES _____
5. STORE _____

A B C D E F G H I J K L M N O P Q R S T U V W X Y Z

Fill in the missing letters. The alphabet has been written out to help you.

Example: AB is to CD as PQ is to <u>RS</u>

6. KN is to OR as VY is to _____
7. JM is to PS as BE is to _____
8. WU is to SQ as JH is to _____
9. TW is to XY as GJ is to _____
10. DW is to GT as JQ is to _____
11. DH is to CD as TX is to _____

Read the first two statements and then underline one of the four options below that must be true.

12. 'Tony loves chocolate bars. Chocco bars are his favourite.'
    A Chocco bars are the only type of chocolate bars that Tony buys.
    B Chocco bars are a type of chocolate bar.
    C Tony's favourites snacks are chocolate bars.
    D Tony eats chocolate bars most days.

13. 'My father catches the train to London every day. Often the train is late.'
    A My father's train is often late.
    B My father is often late for the train.
    C The train to London is late every day.
    D The train from London is often late.

If e=9, f=2, g=10, h=5 and i=0, find the value of the following calculations:

14. $(e + f) \times i =$ _____
15. $\dfrac{g}{h} \times f =$ _____
16. $g^2 + f^2 =$ _____
17. $(h + i) \times (e - f) =$ _____

The next Tuesday after:

18. Wednesday 16th September is _____.
19. Tuesday 27th October is _____.
20. Sunday 29th November is _____.

Test 11: Mixed

Test time: 0 – 5 – 10 minutes

Underline two words, one from each group, that go together to form a new word. The word in the first group always comes first.

Example: (hand, <u>green</u>, for)   (light, <u>house</u>, sure)

1. (where, when, which)   (as, if, over)
2. (climb, stood, dug)   (off, in, out)
3. (by, con, in)   (war, test, low)
4. (low, par, give)   (take, way, many)

Rearrange the letters in capitals to make another word. The new word has something to do with the first two words.

Example: spot, soil   SAINT   STAIN

5. javelin, lance   REAPS   _____
6. stationed, displayed   DESPOT   _____
7. response, reply   CREATION   _____
8. diagram, plan   SINGED   _____
9. broom, sweeper   SHRUB   _____

Underline the word in the brackets which goes best with the words given outside the brackets.

Example: word, paragraph, sentence   (pen, cap, <u>letter</u>, top, stop)

10. suddenly, unexpectedly, abruptly   (soon, loudly, quickly, clearly, mistakenly)
11. deduct, remove, diminish   (divide, decimal, add, subtract, percentage)
12. penalty, forfeit, fine   (goal, game, punishment, reward, rule)
13. fur, fleece, coat   (comb, head, hairstyle, stroke, pelt)
14. chase, hunt, trail   (look, chide, wound, pursue, climb)

Here are some codes for four words. Work out which code matches which word.

# / < ~	# / ~ ~	< / ~ >	~ < / >
PAST	MAPS	MASS	SPAT

15. PAST _____   17. MASS _____
16. MAPS _____   18. SPAT _____

Encode: Decode:

19. STAMP _____   20. ~ < / ~ # _____

TEST 12: **Mixed**

Test time: 0 — 5 — 10 minutes

Underline the two words which are the odd ones out in the following groups of words.

Example: black <u>king</u> purple green <u>house</u>

1	train	track	coach	instruct	rail
2	head	foot	chief	principal	mind
3	crucial	vital	unnecessary	key	lock
4	raspberry	strawberry	peach	cherry	blackberry
5	ask	beg	beseech	implore	query

Find the three-letter word which can be added to the letters in capitals to make a new word. The new word will complete the sentence sensibly.

Example: The cat sprang onto the MO. ____USE____

6 The pirate had a CH over one eye. _____

7 "There is too much CTER in this classroom" said the teacher. _____

8 Red Riding Hood's grandmother lived in a COTT deep in the woods. _____

9 When you FR, your brow wrinkles. _____

10 A rat is a type of ROT. _____

Remove one letter from the word in capital letters to leave a new word. The meaning of the new word is given in the clue.

Example: AUNT   an insect   ____ANT____

11 PLIGHT   illuminate   _____
12 TWINGE   string   _____
13 LEATHER soap   _____
14 HOISTED entertained   _____

Give the two missing numbers in the following sequences.

Example: 2   4   6   <u>8</u>   <u>10</u>

15	19	18	16	___	9	___
16	13	___	19	22	___	28
17	6	7	9	___	___	3
18	___	42	___	28	21	14
19	___	___	20	22	25	27
20	128	___	32	___	8	4

13

Test 13: Mixed

Craig's birthday is on 4th February. Toby's birthday is one week before Craig's and three weeks before Frank's.

1. When is Toby's birthday? _____
2. When is Frank's birthday? _____
3. If I break up from school on Tuesday 29th July and I go back to school on Wednesday 3rd September, how many weeks' holiday do I have? _____
4. How many days altogether in September and October? _____

Benjamin went to the dentist on a Tuesday. He has two further appointments for fillings. One is ten days later, the next is five days after the second appointment. On which days of the week are the following appointments?

5. the second appointment _____
6. the third appointment _____

Find a word that is similar in meaning to the word in capital letters and that rhymes with the second word.

Example: CABLE   tyre   __wire__

7. DISH   roll   _____
8. BENEATH   wonder   _____
9. HORSE   hair   _____
10. AFFLUENT ditch   _____
11. AIM   joint   _____

Rearrange the muddled letters in capitals to make a proper word. The answer will complete the sentence sensibly.

Example: A BEZAR is an animal with stripes.   __ZEBRA__

12. A CHITNEK is a room in a house. _____
13. Would you like a TTSEOAD cheese sandwich? _____
14. Her birthday is on the GTHIEH. _____
15. A GTFHI broke out between the boys. _____
16. This morning it is bright and SFRYOT. _____

Find the letter which will end the first word and start the second word.

Example: peac (h) ome

17. stran (___) ebt
18. fad (___) ats
19. stra (___) hinny
20. thum (___) athe

Test 14: Mixed

Underline the one word in the brackets which will go equally well with both the pairs of words outside the brackets.

Example: rush, attack   cost, fee   (price, hasten, strike, <u>charge</u>, money)

1. lessen, reduce   brighten, illuminate   (decrease, shade, lighten, lose, subtract)
2. opening, break   pierce, puncture   (fissure, hole, perforate, whole, deflate)
3. lord, noble   gape, gaze   (duke, vision, stare, look, peer)
4. coerce, compel   build, construct   (impel, produce, cause, gain, make)
5. head, features   confront, tackle   (handle, object, face, note, manage)

Complete the following sentences by selecting the most sensible word from each group of words given in the brackets. Underline the word selected.

Example: The (<u>children</u>, books, foxes) carried the (houses, <u>books</u>, steps) home from the (greengrocer, <u>library</u>, factory).

6. My baby (caterpillar, bird, brother) crawls down the (lift, stairs, bus) (tomorrow, backwards, table).
7. It has rained so (slowly, little, heavily) the (bus, hill, river) has (flooded, swum, drowned).
8. Please (close, break, open) the (parcel, window, rule), Gavin, as it is (Sunday, cold, noon).
9. When the postman (knocks, eats, smiles) our (cat, clock, dog) (barks, neighs, chimes).

A B C D E F G H I J K L M N O P Q R S T U V W X Y Z

Fill in the missing letters. The alphabet has been written out to help you.

Example: AB is to CD as PQ is to <u>RS</u>

10. LI is to KH as DA is to ____
11. MP is to MJ as FI is to ____
12. QP is to ML as JI is to ____
13. GJ is to FK as QT is to ____
14. MN is to KP as JQ is to ____
15. LH is to OK as PL is to ____

If $u = 16$, $v = 12$, $w = 10$, $j = 5$, $y = 4$ and $z = 2$, find the value of the following calculations. Write your answer as a letter.

16. $(j^2 - u) - y$ = ____
17. $\frac{yw}{j} + z$ = ____
18. $\frac{u + v + y}{z}$ = ____
19. $\frac{(vz + y^2)}{j} + z$ = ____
20. $(6j - 2v) + y$ = ____

TEST 15: **Mixed**

Test time: 0 5 10 minutes

Find a word that can be put in front of each of the following words to make new, compound words.

Example: CAST   FALL   WARD   POUR   __DOWN__

1 BROW   LIGHT   LAND   LIGHTER   _____
2 POWER   GROVE   AGE   HOLE   _____
3 BOW   FIRE   ROADS   BAR   _____
4 MARE   GOWN   CLUB   LIFE   _____

Find and underline the two words which need to change places for the sentence to make sense.

Example: She went to <u>letter</u> the <u>write</u>.

5 He climbed the stairs slowly as he did not go to want to bed.
6 Michelle fell over in her playground and cut the knee badly.
7 Britain's changeable is climate.
8 Blisters can occur when your feet or shoes rub your boots.
9 Tina's mother gives her break to eat at fruit.

The fish counter in my local supermarket is laid out like this:

LEFT   RIGHT

A	B	C	D	E	F

From the information below, work out which type of fish goes into each tray.

The salmon steaks are between the cod and tuna steaks. The sea bream is directly to the left of the cod but to the right of the halibut. The plaice is next to the tuna steaks on the right.

10 salmon   ____   13 sea bream ____
11 cod   ____   14 halibut   ____
12 tuna   ____   15 plaice   ____

If the code for CONSTANTLY is * ! $ £ ^ @ $ ^ > %, decode these words:

16 £ ^ ! $ %   _____   18 $ @ £ ^ %   _____
17 * > @ £ £   _____

Using the same code, encode these words:

19 STOOL   _____   20 COTTON   _____

16

Total

Test 16: Mixed

Underline two words, one from each group, that go together to form a new word. The word in the first group always comes first.

Example: (hand, <u>green</u>, for)   (light, <u>house</u>, sure)

1. (take, name, part)   (more, less, some)
2. (west, hospital, double)   (bed, size, ward)
3. (high, counter, leaf)   (wheel, game, act)
4. (tar, tear, give)   (man, son, get)

A B C D E F G H I J K L M N O P Q R S T U V W X Y Z

5. If the code for SERMON is UGTOQP, what is the code for TALKS? _____
6. If the code for SUBTLE is RTASKD, what is the code for QUICK? _____
7. If the code for PARCEL is SZUBHK, what is the code for GIFTS? _____
8. If the code for ANGELS is ZOFFKT, what is the code for STARS? _____
9. If the code for CHAIRS is YDWENO, what is the code for TABLE? _____

Underline one word in the brackets which is most opposite in meaning to the word in capitals.

Example: WIDE   (broad   vague   long   <u>narrow</u>   motorway)

10. REMEMBER   (recall   recollect   forget   forgive   foretell)
11. CHARM   (repel   captivate   dazzle   enchant   delight)
12. CONFIDENT   (bold   courageous   timid   valiant   vacant)
13. ROUGH   (bumpy   gentle   rowdy   smother   brutal)
14. APPEAR   (emerge   materialise   hide   disappoint   vanish)

Find a word that is similar in meaning to the word in capital letters and that rhymes with the second word.

15. BOTHER   rubble   _____
16. COUNTERFEIT   make   _____
17. GENTLE   wild   _____

Three friends are all taking their driving test in the same month, April. Zita takes it first, nine days before Tony. Zoe takes her test on the second-last day of the month and exactly two weeks after Tony.

18. Zita takes her test on _____.
19. Tony takes his test on _____.
20. Zoe takes her test on _____.

TEST 17: Mixed

Rearrange the muddled letters in capitals to make a proper word. The answer will complete the sentence sensibly.

Example: A BEZAR is an animal with stripes. __ZEBRA__

1. Their school MOUFNIR is green. _____
2. CRUMEYR is the planet closest to the sun. _____
3. You look as if you have been dragged through a DEGHE backwards. _____
4. The city centre was congested with FACTFIR. _____
5. Three times five is TEFFINE. _____

Underline the word in the brackets which goes best with the words given outside the brackets.

Example: word, paragraph, sentence (pen, cap, <u>letter</u>, top, stop)

6. worry, anxiety (relaxed, calmness, peaceful, relieved, apprehension)
7. scenic, picturesque (country, view, sketch, play, attractive)
8. peep, peek (stare, study, temper, glance, gape)
9. bleak, bare (cold, plentiful, stark, clue, abundant)
10. actual, genuine (authentic, fake, false, dishonest, bogus)

Remove one letter from the word in capital letters to leave a new word. The meaning of the new word is given in the clue.

Example: AUNT an insect __ANT__

11. QUITE leave _____
12. BRANCH large farm _____
13. WITCH tickle _____
14. CLAIM mollusc _____

Give the two missing numbers in the following sequences.

Example: 2 4 6 __8__ __10__

15. 2 3 ___ 4 6 ___
16. ___ ___ 20 40 80 160
17. 3 7 11 ___ ___ 23
18. 1 3 6 8 ___ ___
19. 3 ___ 8 4 ___ 6
20. 17 16 ___ 11 7 ___

TEST 18: Mixed

A B C D E F G H I J K L M N O P Q R S T U V W X Y Z

1. If the code for BOTHER is ANSGDQ, what is the code for TRUTH? _____
2. If the code for PRAYER is QSBZFS, what is the code for CHANT? _____
3. If the code for SAILED is UCKNGF, what is the code for YACHT? _____
4. If the code for PENCIL is NCLAGJ, what is the code for RULER? _____
5. If the code for CLUTCH is AMSUAI, what is the code for BRAKE? _____
6. If the code for BOTTLE is ZMRRJC, what is the code for WATER? _____

Underline the two words which are the odd ones out in the following groups of words.

Example: black <u>king</u> purple green <u>house</u>

7. imposing magnificent impostor splendid magnify
8. eye ear knee hip elbow
9. tear cry howl wail noise
10. beat pound pence pancake batter
11. wash bathe basket bowl write

Fill in the crosswords so that all the given words are included. You have been given one letter as a clue in each crossword.

12–15

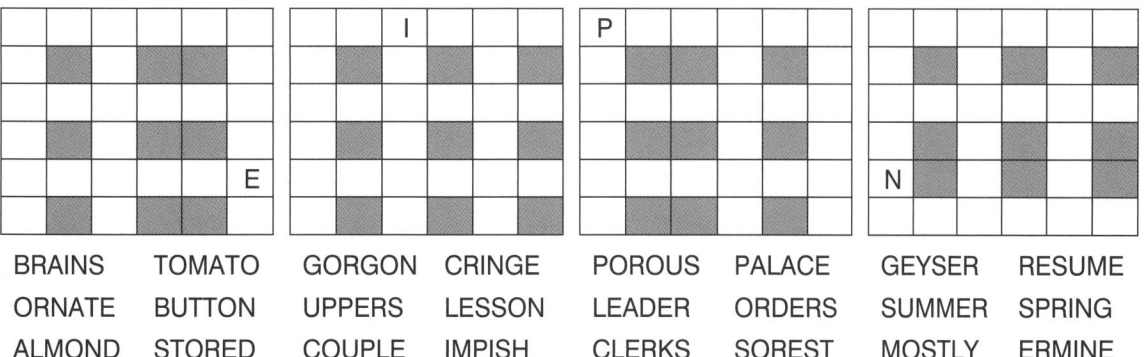

BRAINS	TOMATO	GORGON	CRINGE	POROUS	PALACE	GEYSER	RESUME
ORNATE	BUTTON	UPPERS	LESSON	LEADER	ORDERS	SUMMER	SPRING
ALMOND	STORED	COUPLE	IMPISH	CLERKS	SOREST	MOSTLY	ERMINE

Find the letter which will end the first word and start the second word.

Example: peac (h) ome

16. plan (___) go
17. slan (___) hrow
18. benc (___) orde
19. whar (___) ate
20. medi (___) rime

TEST 19: Mixed

Underline the one word in the brackets which will go equally well with both the pairs of words outside the brackets.

Example: rush, attack   cost, fee   (price, hasten, strike, <u>charge</u>, money)

1   blaze, inferno   shoot, discharge   (flames, fire, launch, gun, burning)
2   delicate, faint   underweight, flimsy   (gentle, soft, light, pale, fade)
3   fleck, spot   celebrate, observe   (speck, stamp, dot, seal, mark)
4   skin, pelt   camouflage, cloak   (hide, lose, conceal, cover, jacket)
5   name, label   shout, cry   (identify, yell, screech, call, brand)

Complete the following sentences in the best way by choosing one word from each set of brackets.

Example: Tall is to (tree, <u>short</u>, colour) as narrow is to (thin, white, <u>wide</u>).

6   Play is to (scene, audience, ticket) as book is to (chapter, cover, author).
7   Wolf is to (dog, pack, wild) as goose is to (feather, beak, flock).
8   Cow is to (milk, farm, bull) as duck is to (feather, drake, fly).
9   Minor is to (age, lesser, main) as favourite is to (preferred, inferior, secondary).

In a code, if A = 1, B = 2, C = 3 and so on, encode these words:

10   HEDGE   _____   12   CABBAGE   _____
11   FACED   _____

Using the same code, decode these:

13   31754   _____   15   21475   _____
14   61454   _____

Find and underline the two words which need to change places for the sentence to make sense.

Example: She went to <u>letter</u> the <u>write</u>.

16   At the weekend we often have gravy meat, vegetables and roast.
17   My father ate her lunch with my aunt in the garden.
18   As the storm raged, the rocks crashed against the waves.
19   Twickenham is the rugby of English home.
20   My grandmother's chime has a very loud clock.

TEST 20: **Mixed**

Test time: 0 5 10 minutes

Find a word that can be put in front of each of the following words to make new, compound words.

Example: CAST   FALL   WARD   POUR   ___DOWN___

1	SOME	SHAKE	CUFF	WRITING	_____
2	BURST	SIDE	LINE	BREAK	_____
3	SHED	WIND	WORK	PECKER	_____
4	BOAT	STYLE	TIME	LINE	_____

Change the first word of the third pair in the same way as the other pairs to give a new word.

Example: bind, hind   bare, hare   but, ___hut___

5	dark, bark	drain, brain	drake, _____
6	cram, arm	hilt, lit	test, _____
7	castanets, cats	cartridge, cage	carbonise, _____
8	society, cosy	crash, arch	mature, _____
9	stencil, nets	stellar, lets	stepfather, _____

If the code for VEGETABLE is 938316253, decode the following words:

10   265531   _____
11   96593   _____

Using the same code, encode these words:

12   BLEAT   _____
13   GABLE   _____
14   LEAVE   _____

Work out the following codes.

15   If the code for SWITCH is TXJUDI, what does DMBNQ stand for?   _____
16   If the code for BEETLE is ADDSKD, what does VNQLR stand for?   _____
17   If the code for TREATS is VTGCVU, what does VWTPU stand for?   _____
18   If the code for WASHES is UYQFCQ, what is the code for BASIN?   _____
19   If the code for DREAMS is FQGZOR, what is the code for SIZES?   _____
20   If the code for BEATEN is ZFYUCO, what is the code for SORRY?   _____

21

TEST 21: Mixed

Underline the pair of words most opposite in meaning.

Example: cup, mug   coffee, milk   hot, cold

1	neglect, nurture	strike, knock	ignore, overlook
2	doubtful, distrustful	trusting, wary	dubious, suspect
3	basin, bath	float, sink	hot, warm
4	many, few	numerous, plentiful	best, finest

Look at the first group of three words. The word in the middle has been made from the other two words. Complete the second group of three words in the same way, making a new word in the middle.

Example: PAIN   INTO   TOOK   ALSO   __SOON__   ONLY

5	WANT	SENT	SEAL	MOTH	_____	PALE
6	PACE	PART	TRIM	FLIP	_____	WEST
7	SOON	SIGN	HIGH	FEET	_____	LACE
8	KILN	KIND	NEED	SUCH	_____	ROPE
9	HINT	THIN	HAND	HARP	_____	RAYS

Underline the word in the brackets which goes best with the words given outside the brackets.

Example: word, paragraph, sentence   (pen, cap, letter, top, stop)

10	gentle, mild	(rough, placid, extreme, forceful, violent)
11	muddle, tangle	(organised, jumble, structured, tidy, neat)
12	house, bungalow	(castle, palace, mansion, hotel, cottage)
13	sodden, drenched	(burnt, scorched, soaked, damp, dry)
14	previous, former	(later, subsequent, next, prior, last)

A B C D E F G H I J K L M N O P Q R S T U V W X Y Z

Give the missing letters and numbers in the following sequences. The alphabet has been written out to help you.

Example: CQ   DQ   EP   FP   GO   HO

15	____	Rs8	Pu7	____	Ly5	Ja4
16	JCA	KCC	____	KDG	____	KDK
17	MN	____	KP	____	IR	HS
18	bde	fhi	____	npq	____	vxy
19	25A	____	17Y	13X	9W	____
20	____	TZ	WY	ZX	____	FV

TEST 22: **Mixed**

Test time: 0　5　10 minutes

Find and underline the two words which need to change places for the sentence to make sense.

Example:　She went to <u>letter</u> the <u>write</u>.

1　On Friday night, Peter to going is the cinema.
2　My father straightens the tie in front of his hall mirror.
3　The traffic led as the duck stopped her ducklings across the road.
4　In school, we play football after the park.
5　In the distance, I could see a hot sky balloon high in the air.

Underline the two words which are the odd ones out in the following groups of words.

Example:　black　<u>king</u>　purple　green　<u>house</u>

6　petrol　　cap　　　bonnet　　wheel　　beret
7　find　　　weigh　　track　　　follow　　trail
8　below　　beneath　between　beyond　under
9　pass　　　grade　　fail　　　　rank　　　rate
10　sporadic　often　　infrequent　periodic　regular

Move one letter from the first word and add it to the second word to make two new words.

Example:　hunt　sip　　　__hut__　　　__snip__

11　grasping　fail　　　_____　_____
12　rare　　　pawns　　_____　_____
13　splint　　wader　　_____　_____
14　finger　　thin　　　_____　_____

Give the two missing numbers in the following sequences.

Example:　2　4　6　__8__　__10__

15　2　　11　　4　　___　　6　　5　　___　　2
16　13　　___　　16　　17　　19　　___　　22　　23
17　___　　2　　___　　7　　11　　16
18　8　　11　　___　　17　　___　　23
19　96　　48　　24　　___　　6　　___
20　15　　___　　11　　7　　___　　4　　3　　1

TEST 23: **Mixed**

Test time: 0 — 5 — 10 minutes

My grandmother's sewing box has nine compartments. The cottons are in the top right and the middle left compartments. The pins are in the bottom middle one. Work out where the other items go:

TOP

1	2	3 Cottons
4 Cottons	5	6
7	8 Pins	9

BOTTOM

My grandmother kept the needles next to the pins and the thimble above the needles. The tape measure is not next to the pins. The folding scissors are above one of the cotton compartments. The buttons are not next to the needles. The pincushion is kept above the pins and next to one of the cottons.

1 needles ___   3 tape measure ___   5 buttons   ___
2 thimble ___   4 scissors   ___   6 pincushion ___

Underline the word in the brackets which is most opposite in meaning to the word in capitals.

Example: WIDE   (broad   vague   long   <u>narrow</u>   motorway)

7   APPRECIATE   (neglect   prize   esteem   respect   value)
8   TIDY   (neat   messy   seaside   orderly   untied)
9   TIRED   (wheel   exhausted sleepy   stale   rested)
10 AMIABLE   (friendly   unfriendly kind   agreeable affable)
11 WONDERFUL   (fabulous   fantastic dreadful amazing   joyous)

A B C D E F G H I J K L M N O P Q R S T U V W X Y Z

12   If the code for BATTER is ^ @ / / = £, decode ^ = / / = £.   _____
13   If the code for TREBLE is 748918, decode 98487.   _____
14   If the code for WINTER is XJPQFN, decode NFPFX.   _____
15   If the code for CRADLE is ~ @ / # ? !, decode ? / @ # ! @.   _____
16   If the code for FASTER is ! I 7 4 $ X, decode 7 I ! $ X.   _____

Find the letter which will complete both pairs of words, ending the first word and starting the second. The same letter must be used for both sets of words.

Example: mea (t) able   fi (t) ub

17   tin   (___) awn   part   (___) ellow
18   tea   (___) ight   cella (___) ode
19   war   (___) ought   bee   (___) oun
20   bras (___) ire   peris (___) ound

24

Total

Answers

Bond 10 Minute Tests Verbal Reasoning 11+–12+

Test 1: Sorting Words 1

1 gossip
2 invent
3 precise
4 disgrace
5 protect
6 eager, enthusiastic
7 crisis, dilemma
8 charge, entrust
9 perish, die
10 enrage, infuriate
11 mouldy
12 jealousy
13 rough
14 swirl
15 admire
16 twitter, babble
17 glimmer, glitter
18 type, category
19 sumptuous, luxurious
20 peckish, hungry

Test 2: Sorting Words 2

1 pedestrian, car
2 gush, pour
3 consider, think
4 gift, present
5 awkward, bulky
6 bold
7 cover
8 image
9 lie
10 train
11 flight
12 flame
13 bought
14 climb
15 doubt
16 heavy
17 ordinary
18 help
19 present
20 near

Test 3: Selecting Words 1

1 chopstick
2 outlaw
3 oatmeal
4 highland
5 BACK
6 FLASH
7 WIND
8 SUN
9 g
10 t
11 m
12 p
13 disapprove
14 distribute
15 minute
16 novel
17 revolt, support
18 assemble, dismantle
19 imperfect, flawless
20 benefit, handicap

Test 4: Selecting Words 2

1 b
2 e
3 c
4 f
5 ee
6 th
7 ch
8 le

Test 5: Anagrams 1

1 SPARSE
2 DINES
3 DESPAIR
4 STAPLE
5 EQUIP
6 LEVER
7 One, she
8 green, blue
9 room, children
10 sitting, carpet
11 outside, hard
12 you, I
13 STUN
14 TRIP
15 PART
16 BLUE
17 BOTH
18 PITY
19 BRAY
20 POLE

Test 6: Anagrams 2

1 they
2 told
3 near
4 sour
5 shun
6 scar
7 note
8 vest
9 LID
10 BAG
11 LAY
12 TEN
13 RAN
14 MET
15 HARM
16 WING
17 NEST
18 RATE
19 PORT
20 TIME

Test 7: Coded Sequences and Logic 1

1 CE
2 TB
3 RU
4 AX
5 IR
6 RF, SB
7 gR, mN
8 A6, C8
9 17T, 13S
10 YE, AG
11 5, 17
12 4, 16
13 23, 20
14 16, 26
15 14, 21
16 b
17 d
18 b
19 c
20 a

Test 8: Coded Sequences and Logic 2

1 XA
2 JQ
3 VX
4 XT
5 MN
6 Y5, C25
7 RP, SQ
8 11l, 13K
9 AZ, DW
10 cLd, iRj
11 52, 48
12 11, 17
13 46, 39
14 4, 13
15 12, 96
16 CRAFT
17 TWEED
11 SPOON
12 TIRED
13 patent, brain
14 wing, swarm
15 paring, knight
16 breath, spine
17 CROP, COOP
18 KNOT, KNIT
19 SPUN, SPUR
20 MACE, MICE

Test 9: Coded Sequences and Logic 3

1 BARE
2 NEAR
3 BEAN
4 BARN
5 * ^ 3 6
6 ^ 3 * 6 ^
7 FKEGF
8 TQFFE
9 LMRCQ
10 RVHRG
11 A = lettuces
12 B = radishes
13 C = spinach
14 E = peas
15 F = onions
16 G = herbs
17 2nd
18 Monday
19 26th
20 Saturday

Test 10: Coded Sequences and Logic 4

1 19
2 20
3 25
4 22
5 25
6 ZC
7 HK
8 FD
9 KL
10 MN
11 ST
12 B
13 A
14 0
15 4
16 104
17 35
18 22nd September
19 3rd November
20 1st December

Test 11: Mixed

1 whereas
2 dugout
3 contest
4 partake
5 SPEAR
6 POSTED
7 REACTION
8 DESIGN
9 BRUSH
10 quickly
11 subtract
12 punishment
13 pelt
14 pursue
15 < / ~ >
16 # / < ~
17 # / ~ ~
18 ~ < / >
19 ~ > / # <
20 SPASM

Test 12: Mixed

1 track, rail
2 foot, mind
3 unnecessary, lock
4 peach, cherry
5 ask, query
6 PAT
7 HAT
8 AGE
9 OWN
10 DEN
11 LIGHT
12 TWINE
13 LATHER
14 HOSTED

Bond 10 Minute Tests Verbal Reasoning 11⁺–12⁺

14 HOSTED
15 13, 4
16 16, 25
17 5, 12
18 49, 35
19 15, 17
20 64, 16

Test 13: Mixed

1 28th January
2 18th February
3 5
4 61
5 Friday
6 Wednesday
7 bowl
8 under
9 mare
10 rich
11 point
12 KITCHEN
13 TOASTED
14 EIGHTH
15 FIGHT
16 FROSTY
17 d
18 e
19 w
20 b

Test 14: Mixed

1 lighten
2 hole
3 peer
4 make
5 face
6 brother, stairs, backwards
7 heavily, river, flooded
8 close, window, cold
9 knocks, dog, barks
10 CZ
11 FC
12 FE
13 PU
14 HS
15 SO
16 j
17 w
18 u
19 w
20 w

Test 15: Mixed

1 HIGH
2 MAN
3 CROSS
4 NIGHT
5 go, want
6 her, the
7 changeable, climate
8 feet, boots
9 break, fruit
10 D
11 C
12 E
13 B
14 A
15 F
16 STONY
17 CLASS
18 NASTY
19 £ ^ ! ! >
20 * ! ^ ^ ! $

Test 16: Mixed

1 nameless
2 westward
3 counteract
4 target
5 VCNMU
6 PTHBJ
7 JHISV
8 RUZSR
9 PWXHA
10 forget
11 repel
12 timid

13 gentle
14 vanish
15 trouble
16 fake
17 mild
18 6th April
19 15th April
20 29th April

Test 17: Mixed

1 UNIFORM
2 MERCURY
3 HEDGE
4 TRAFFIC
5 FIFTEEN
6 apprehension
7 attractive
8 glance
9 stark
10 authentic
11 QUIT
12 RANCH
13 ITCH
14 CLAM
15 4, 5
16 5, 10
17 15, 19
18 11, 13
19 2, 13
20 14, 2

Test 18: Mixed

1 SQTSG
2 DIBOU
3 ACEJV
4 PSJCP
5 ZSYLC
6 UYRCP
7 impostor, magnify
8 eye, ear
9 tear, noise
10 pence, pancake
11 basket, bowl

13

C	R	I	N	G	E
O		M		O	
U	P	P	E	R	S
P		I		G	
L	E	S	S	O	N
E		H		N	

14

P	O	R	O	U	S
A		R		O	
L	E	A	D	E	R
A		E		E	
C	L	E	R	K	S
E		S		T	

15

S	U	M	M	E	R
P		O		R	
R	E	S	U	M	E
I		T		I	
N		L		N	
G	E	Y	S	E	R

12

B	R	A	I	N	S
U		L		T	
T	O	M	A	T	O
T		O		R	
O	R	N	A	T	E
N		D		D	

16 e
17 t
18 h
19 f
20 c

Test 19: Mixed

1 fire
2 light
3 mark
4 hide
5 call
6 scene, chapter
7 pack, flock
8 bull, drake
9 lesser, preferred
10 85475
11 61354
12 3122175
13 CAGED
14 FADED
15 BADGE
16 gravy, roast

17 father, aunt
18 rocks, waves
19 rugby, home
20 chime, clock

Test 20: Mixed

1 HAND
2 OUT
3 WOOD
4 LIFE
5 brake
6 set
7 case
8 tame
9 pets
10 BALLET
11 VALVE
12 25361
13 86253
14 53693
15 CLAMP
16 WORMS
17 TURNS
18 ZYQGL
19 UHBDU
20 QPPSW

Test 21: Mixed

1 neglect, nurture
2 trusting, wary
3 float, sink
4 many, few
5 PATH
6 FLEW
7 FACT
8 SURE
9 PRAY
10 placid
11 jumble
12 cottage
13 soaked
14 prior
15 Tq9, Nw6
16 JCE, JDI
17 LO, JQ
18 jlm, rtu
19 21Z, 5V
20 QA, CW

Test 22: Mixed

1 to, is
2 the, his
3 led, stopped
4 in, after
5 sky, air
6 petrol, wheel
7 find, weigh
8 between, beyond
9 pass, fail
10 often, regular
11 gasping, frail
12 are, prawns
13 split, wander
14 finer, thing
15 8, 8
16 14, 20
17 1, 4
18 14, 20
19 12, 3
20 10, 7

Test 23: Mixed

1 9   4   1
2 6   5   7
3 2   6   5
7 neglect
8 messy
9 rested
10 unfriendly
11 dreadful
12 BETTER
13 BERET
14 RENEW
15 LARDER
16 SAFER
17 y
18 r
19 n
20 h

A2

Bond 10 Minute Tests Verbal Reasoning 11⁺–12⁺

Test 24: Mixed

1 DESIRE
2 DESERT
3 VERSE
4 RESIST
5 THROB
6 beat, drum
7 criticise, disapprove
8 essential, necessary
9 band, strip
10 17X, 5A
11 IJL, QRT
12 YVX, YWP
13 FU, DW
14 yDb, tSg
15 JPG, HOA
16 c
17 d
18 e
19 f
20 c

Test 25: Mixed

1 l
2 r
3 f
4 t
5 RATE
6 NEST
7 BIRD
8 PASS
9 FLEA
10 EQCEJ
11 KXHMF
12 KNEAB
13 BALLS
14 THUMB
15 SALAD
16 crack
17 cover
18 concern
19 sweet
20 simple

Test 26: Mixed

1 carpet, curtain
2 compress, evolve
3 shirt, trousers
4 balance, evenness
5 pole
6 hide
7 charge
8 swell
9 highly
10 EAR
11 HAS
12 ARM
13 PEA
14 RAG
15 Wednesday
16 Monday
17 31
18 28
19 59 years
20 1991

Test 27: Mixed

1 moth
2 them
3 real
4 meat
5 rate
6 prize, appreciate
7 angle, viewpoint
8 cringe, squirm
9 crook, criminal
10 exit, outlet
11 plant, wiring
12 raid, stable
13 sink, trumps
14 hanged, witch
15 TRUST
16 STUDIES
17 STIFF
18 OPENS
19 ASHES
20 BRAVE

Test 28: Mixed

1 JI
2 BY
3 OR
4 JQ
5 RS
6 TP
7 surround
8 vanish
9 inquisitive
10 perform
11 moveable
12 SLUMP
13 RESIGN
14 TOAST
15 RESPECT
16 SLIME
17 6pm, out, friends
18 gallery, variety, sculptures
19 brother, exam, party
20 eat, fruit, day

Test 29: Mixed

1 WORDS
2 TROUT
3 JUICE
4 WATCH
5 SNOWS
6 blood, animal
7 lick, tongue
8 sentence, paragraph
9 ice, hail
10 8P
11 8J
12 8C
13 8Z
14 8A
15 8T
16 control, curb
17 tip, point
18 eagerness, zeal
19 lighten, reduce
20 aloof, distant

Test 30: Mixed

1 b
2 w
3 s
4 p
5–8

B	E	E	T	L	E
R		X		A	
E	N	T	E	R	S
A		R		D	
T	R	A	D	E	R
H		S		R	

P	A	R	E	N	T
O		E		H	
O	F	F	I	C	E
D		I		I	
L	A	N	C	E	R
E		E		S	

N	E	T	T	L	E
O		E		I	
D	R	A	I	N	S
U		S		E	
L		E		R	
E	L	D	E	S	T

C	R	U	M	B	S
A		S		R	
N	E	E	D	E	D
O		F		A	
P	O	U	N	D	S
Y		L		S	

9 7U, 5A
10 If, Kg
11 UGG, TIH
12 RX, XA
13 NOG, LPI
14 EV, IR
15 15
16 24
17 26
18 12
19 18
20 23

Test 31: Mixed

1 summit, base
2 torrent, trickle
3 truly, falsely
4 robust, sickly
5 peculiar, odd
6 note, observe
7 thrifty, frugal
8 perch, sit
9 swivel, turn
10 TALKS
11 CARDS
12 CLAIM
13 DIZZY
14 HAPPY
15 2nd April
16 10th April
17 4th June
18 5th July
19 C
20 C

Test 32: Mixed

1 JANUARY
2 ICEBERG
3 TWICE
4 ENDED
5 BISCUITS
6 madden
7 critic
8 value
9 stifle
10 joint
11 WISH, FISH
12 GRIP, DRIP
13 GULL, GALL
14 PINE, PANE
15 13, 7
16 10, 8
17 5, 12
18 12, 16
19 11, 23
20 4, 32

Test 33: Mixed

1-2 9ᵗʰ January, 30ᵗʰ January
3-4 11, 48
5 50
6 08:28
7 08:45
8–11

D	A	3	K	E	T
A		I		A	
T		T		N	
T	A	R	T	A	N
E		E			
R	U	N	N	E	R

S	T	O	R	M	S
		E		I	
S	M	O	O	T	H
		P		T	
		T		E	
R	E	D	E	E	M
		R			

W	I	N	T	E	R
I		I		E	
L	A	T	E	S	T
L		R		U	
O		O		R	
W	O	O	D	E	N

E	M	E	R	G	E
X		O		O	
I	M	A	G	E	S
S		U		A	
T		T		Y	
S	E	N	S	E	S

12 @ 8 a ^ ?
13 t u p o
14 # ~ ! > /
15 a n s u r
16 ~ $ # ~ %
17 it
18 sh
19 ut
20 ap

Test 34: Mixed

1 tense
2 fix
3 coast
4 weird
5 stay
6 gravel, tarmac
7 still, active
8 distant, far
9 compete, fight
10 SQ
11 QR
12 YX

Bond 10 Minute Tests Verbal Reasoning 11+–12+

13 KN
14 WT
15 KP
16 witch
17 lit
18 tone
19 chat
20 her

Test 35: Mixed

1 FRAIL
2 PLEATED
3 CROUCH
4 PRIDE
5 shed
6 mean
7 scan
8 vent
9 then
10 TABLE
11 SEVEN
12 FIGHT
13 EDDBK
14 IPMFT
15 ECTTA
16 flourish, thrive
17 life, existence
18 blank, clear
19 candid, frank
20 signal, gesture

Test 36: Mixed

1 start, conclude
2 question, reply
3 over, under
4 upright, reclined
5 2   8 18
6 10 9 70
7 33
10 entire, complete
11 part, split
12 hillock, mound
13 yap, bark
14 swamp, marsh
15 FA, ID
16 3B, 9K
17 qF, mJ
18 IR, JQ
19 GT4, UU2
20 BHO, DLM

Test 37: Mixed

1 sick, nauseous
2 ponder, contemplate
3 paw, foot
4 depress, sadden
5 crime, offence
6 THIN
7 STOP
8 FAST
9 PACE
10 FILE
11 HARM, HARP
12 LAZE, LAME
13 REED, READ
14 PEAT, MEAT
15 RQRRA
16 GZTSJ
17 TIXET
18 CARRY
19 SMALL
20 SUGAR

Test 38: Mixed

1 14, 19
2 2, 6
3 3, 9
4 10, 22
5 4, 32
6 4, 5

7 gate
8 bear
9 also
10 tool
11 scar
12 clap
13 flourish
14 tetchy
15 hamper
16 crowd
17 be   19 el
18 st   20 gn

Test 39: Mixed

1 reed
2 net
3 link
4 rot
5 ten
6 country, city
7 skin, tooth
8 brush, comb
9 estimate, outline
10 BACK
11 KNEE
12 JERK
13 SZOU
14 DLIW
15 BZDM
16 bold
17 sensible
18 complex
19 many
20 fleeting

Test 40: Mixed

1 PLANET
2 CASTLE
3 BEACH
4 FLATTER
5 PASS
6 PORT
7 HOLE
8 LEND
9 PAIR
10 FZQCB
11 JSLAF
12 ZSCPX
13 ZEBRA
14 BEANS
15 HUTCH
16 oak
17 beech
18 maple
19 ash
20 sycamore

Puzzle ❶

Leeds
London
Bristol

Puzzle ❷

WILD
LIFE CAT
BOAT GUARD FISH
MAN ROOM EYE FINGER
AGE DRILL PIECE BALL NAIL
SPAR OLD WORK ROOM POINT FILE
ROW RING HORSE PLACE FULL LESS FAN
WING LET PLAY FIELD MAT FILL STAR SING
BEAT BACK WORK MOUSE CUP UP GIRL
TEN HAND FORCE HOLE TIE GUARD
DON SOME NINE UP LINE
KEY WHERE TEEN EAR
AS FORE THEN
UNDER EVER
FOOT
WEAR BALL
OUT LOON COCK
WARD BOAT ATTIC TAIL
DEN GAME LOFT GATE OR
NOTE TASTE TEA HOUSE RANGE BIT
LET BLACK BUD BOUND TRAIN HEAVY TEN
HALL SPOT DING LESS NURSE LOAD DEER ANT
MARK ASK ON MAID DEAD SKIN THEM
KING SET LINE WEIGHT HEAD SELF
DOME TEE DANCE SHIP FISH
TOTAL THE FLOOR BONE
REIN ME PICK
DEER AN
GEL

Puzzle ❸

The treasure of Black Jack lies under the palm tree in the north of Dead Man's Island. X marks the spot. The X should be placed on the palm tree at the top of the map.

Puzzle ❹

G	R	O	W	S		E	A	G	E	R
R			O		N					A
I			R		R					G
N		E	R	R	O	R				G
S	U	N	N	Y		L	I	T	H	E
		T				F				
T	O	W	E	L		F	L	A	M	E
O			R	O	G	U	E			P
A				G		D				O
S				I		G				C
T	O	N	I	C		E	A	R	T	H

Puzzle ❺

LADY	EVENT	RELATIONSHIP	PLACE
Miss Millard	Tennis tournament	schoolchildren	Godalming
Miss Jones	Tea	Niece	Guildford
Mrs Pringle	Sunday lunch	Grandchildren	Surbiton
Mrs Prout	Nature ramble	Husband	Redhill
Mrs Snape	Swimming	Friend	Richmond

Test 24: Mixed

Rearrange the letters in capitals to make another word. The new word has something to do with the first two words.

Example: spot   soil   SAINT   __STAIN__

1. wish, fancy — RESIDE — _____
2. abandon, leave — RESTED — _____
3. poem, lyric — SERVE — _____
4. endure, withstand — SISTER — _____
5. pulse, thump — BROTH — _____

Choose two words, one from each set of brackets, to complete the sentence in the best way.

Example: Smile is to happiness as (drink, <u>tear</u>, shout) is to (whisper, laugh, <u>sorrow</u>).

6. Blow is to trumpet as (call, beat, tap) is to (piano, drum, names).
7. Grumble is to complain as (speak, reply, criticise) is to (support, disapprove, encourage).
8. Require is to need as (essential, reject, consider) is to (necessary, hopeful, happy).
9. Belt is to strap as (group, musicians, band) is to (strip, flag, poster).

A B C D E F G H I J K L M N O P Q R S T U V W X Y Z

Give the missing letters and numbers in the following sequences. The alphabet has been written out to help you.

Example: CQ   DQ   EP   FP   <u>GO</u>   <u>HO</u>

10. ____   5Y   17Z   ____   17B   5C
11. ABD   EFH   ____   MNP   ____   UVX
12. XVZ   ____   XVV   YWT   XWR   ____
13. HS   GT   ____   EV   ____   CX
14. ____   xGc   wJd   vMe   uPf   ____
15. KOJ   ____   IQD   ____   GPX   FQU

If a = 5, b = 3, c = 10, d = 2, e = 20 and f = 4, find the value of the following calculations. Write your answer as a letter.

16. $(a^2 - e) \times d = $ ____
17. $\dfrac{2e - bc}{a} = $ ____
18. $\left(\dfrac{3c}{b}\right) \times d = $ ____
19. $(4b - c) + d = $ ____
20. $\dfrac{bc}{a} + f = $ ____

TEST 25: Mixed

Which one letter can be added to the front of all these words to make new words?

Example: ___are ___at ___rate ___all **c**

1 ___ever ___adder ___ease ___ink ___
2 ___ant ___eel ___oast ___each ___
3 ___rank ___lute ___able ___inch ___
4 ___each ___race ___ouch ___win ___

Look at the first group of three words. The word in the middle has been made from the other two words. Complete the second group of three words in the same way, making a new word in the middle.

Example: PAIN INTO TOOK ALSO __SOON__ ONLY

5 PARK PALE LEFT RAIL _____ TERM
6 DUMB DRAB GRAM NEWT _____ DESK
7 BILE BLUR USER BAIL _____ RIND
8 BOND FIND FILL FUSS _____ PACT
9 RARE REED BEDS FOOL _____ DEAR

A B C D E F G H I J K L M N O P Q R S T U V W X Y Z

10 If the code for TRAINS is VTCKPU, what is the code for COACH? _____
11 If the code for HONEST is GNMDRS, what is the code for LYING? _____
12 If the code for HORSES is KNURHR, what is the code for HOBBY? _____
13 If the code for TENNIS is PAJJEO, what is XWHHO? _____
14 If the code for FINGER is DJLHCS, what is RISNZ? _____
15 If the code for CARROT is ZXOOLQ, what is PXIXA? _____

Underline the one word in the brackets which will go equally well with both the pairs of words outside the brackets.

Example: rush, attack cost, fee (price, hasten, strike, <u>charge</u>, money)

16 collapse, crumble cleft, crevice (hole, scratch, fall, fissure, crack)
17 cloak, screen insure, protect (underwrite, cover, lid, coat, conceal)
18 involve, affect worry, anxiety (unease, turn, effect, problem, concern)
19 pudding, dessert kind, pleasant (perfumed, good, smelly, sweet, adorable)
20 easy, effortless clear, plain (patterned, simple, natural, transparent, pure)

Test 26: Mixed

Complete the following sentences in the best way by choosing one word from each set of brackets.

Example: Tall is to (tree, <u>short</u>, colour) as narrow is to (thin, white, <u>wide</u>).

1. Floor is to (kitchen, carpet, ceiling) as window is to (curtain, pane, glass).
2. Compact is to (expand, compress, stretch) as develop is to (contract, shorten, evolve).
3. Button is to (chocolate, switch, shirt) as zip is to (leg, trousers, code).
4. Symmetry is to (balance, sides, shapes) as equality is to (inconsistency, evenness, irregularity).

Find a word that is similar to the word in capital letters and that rhymes with the second word.

Example: CABLE   tyre   <u>wire</u>

5. STAFF   roll   _____
6. CONCEAL   lied   _____
7. RUSH   large   _____
8. BULGE   bell   _____
9. GREATLY   smiley   _____

Find the three-letter word which can be added to the letters in capitals to make a new word. The new word will complete the sentence sensibly.

Example: The cat sprang onto the MO.   <u>USE</u>

10. The ace of HTS is a playing card.   _____
11. The dog CED the cat up a tree.   _____
12. The WTH from the fire filled the whole room.   _____
13. The magician made the rabbit APR from nowhere.   _____
14. Please don't ENCOUE him to misbehave.   _____

Matthew, Helen and Emma all have Music exams. Helen's exam is on Thursday 17th June. Matthew's exam is 8 days before Helen's and Emma's is 11 days after Helen's. On which days of the week do Matthew's and Emma's exams fall?

15. Matthew   _____
16. Emma   _____

Three generations of the Thomas family were born in 1935, 1966 and 1994.

17. How old was the grandfather when the father was born?   _____
18. How old was the father when his son was born?   _____
19. What is the age difference between the grandfather and the grandson?   _____
20. The grandson has a sister who is 3 years older. She was born in   _____?

TEST 27: **Mixed**

Test time: 0   5   10 minutes

Find the four-letter word hidden at the end of one word and the beginning of the next word. The order of the letters may not be changed.

Example: The children had ba<u>ts an</u>d balls.   ___sand___

1 Please help him otherwise we will be here for hours.   _____
2 The horse rider crossed the main road carefully.   _____
3 There always seems to be a problem.   _____
4 Come quickly and meet me at the bus stop.   _____
5 The caterpillar ate the cabbage leaf hungrily.   _____

Underline the two words, one from each group, which are closest in meaning.

Example: (race, shop, <u>start</u>)   (finish, <u>begin</u>, end)

6 (winner, prize, valuable)   (appreciate, grow, extensive)
7 (angle, line, direction)   (triangle, viewpoint, degree)
8 (cringe, crimson, critic)   (subtle, squat, squirm)
9 (crutch, crook, stick)   (invalid, old man, criminal)
10 (door, entrance, exit)   (gate, outlet, fence)

Move one letter from the first word and add it to the second word to make two new words.

Example: hunt   sip   ___hut___   ___snip___

11 pliant   wring   _____   _____
12 braid   stale   _____   _____
13 stink   rumps   _____   _____
14 changed   with   _____   _____

A B C D E F G H I J K L M N O P Q R S T U V W X Y Z

15 If the code for DUSTER is 748310, decode 30483.   _____
16 If the code for DUTIES is 135429, decode 9531429.   _____
17 If the code for FIGHTS is o u a y e i, decode i e u o o.   _____
18 If the code for SPOKEN is 8 4 ^ J Z ?, decode ^ 4 Z ? 8.   _____
19 If the code for WASHES is U e 7 4 # 7, decode e 7 4 # 7.   _____
20 If the code for VERBAL is / > £ 6 X !, decode 6 £ X / >.   _____

Total

Test 28: Mixed

A B C D E F G H I J K L M N O P Q R S T U V W X Y Z

Fill in the missing letters. The alphabet has been written out to help you.

Example: AB is to CD as PQ is to RS

1. ZY is to SR as QP is to ____
2. EB is to AX as FC is to ____
3. BC is to AD as PQ is to ____
4. BY is to EV as GT is to ____
5. FJ is to EF as SW is to ____
6. KO is to KG as TX is to ____

Underline the word in brackets closest in meaning to the word in capitals.

Example: UNHAPPY (unkind   death   laughter   <u>sad</u>   friendly)

7. ENVELOP (letter   surround   packet   parcel   stamp)
8. DISAPPEAR (emerge   materialise   appear   vanish   attend)
9. CURIOUS (ordinary   crafty   inquisitive   careful   imaginative)
10. EXECUTE (watch   perform   guard   scrutinise   search)
11. MOBILE (stationary   static   motionless   inactive   moveable)

Rearrange the letters in capitals to make another word. The new word has something to do with the first two words.

Example: spot   soil   SAINT   STAIN

12. slouch, sprawl   PLUMS   _____
13. leave, quit   SINGER   _____
14. pledge, salute   STOAT   _____
15. regard, admiration   SPECTRE   _____
16. sludge, ooze   MILES   _____

Complete the following sentences by selecting the most sensible word from each group of words given in the brackets. Underline the words selected.

Example: The (<u>children</u>, books, foxes) carried the (houses, <u>books</u>, steps) home from the (greengrocer, <u>library</u>, factory).

17. At (noon, 7 am, 6 pm) we are going (by, out, from) to supper with some (friends, homework, elephants).
18. The art (hospital, station, gallery) was filled with a wide (avenue, staircase, variety) of pictures and (sculptures, taxis, animals).
19. Neil's (brother, sister, grandfather) was busy revising for his (exam, holiday, school) so couldn't go to the (house, car, party).
20. Katie knows she should (eat, sleep, weigh) at least five portions of (bread, milk, fruit) and vegetables every (month, minute, day).

TEST 29: **Mixed**

Test time: 0   5   10 minutes

A B C D E F G H I J K L M N O P Q R S T U V W X Y Z

1 If the code for SPEECH is VOHDFG, what is ZNUCV? _____
2 If the code for FISHED is DGQFCB, what is RPMSR? _____
3 If the code for ORANGE is KNWJCA, what is FQEYA? _____
4 If the code for LISTEN is OIVTHN, what is ZAWCK? _____
5 If the code for WINTER is YGPRGP, what is ULQUU? _____

Choose two words, one from each set of brackets, to complete the sentence in the best way.

Example: Smile is to happiness as (drink, <u>tear</u>, shout) is to (whisper, laugh, <u>sorrow</u>).

6 Sap is to tree as (skin, blood, water) is to (nose, animal, river).
7 Chew is to teeth as (walk, blink, lick) is to (tongue, nose, lips).
8 Letter is to word as (idea, punctuation, sentence) is to (chapter, paragraph, page).
9 Water is to rain as (fire, yellow, ice) is to (rainbow, hail, sunshine).

All six classrooms for Year 8 are on the same corridor.
Work out from the information below, which class has which room.

1		3		5

CORRIDOR

6	7	8		

Class 8P is directly opposite 8Z. Class 8A is between 8Z and 8T. Class 8C is not opposite another Year 8 class. Class 8J is in the middle of a row.

10 Room 1 _____   13 Room 6 _____
11 Room 3 _____   14 Room 7 _____
12 Room 5 _____   15 Room 8 _____

Underline the pair of words most similar in meaning.

Example: come, go   <u>roam, wander</u>   fear, fare

16 control, curb   hold, carry   restrain, remain
17 tip, point   strange, normal   clever, idiotic
18 enthusiastic, indifferent   eagerness, zeal   grave, minor
19 lighten, reduce   bright, dark   relaxed, tense
20 smile, sneer   gracious, unkind   aloof, distant

Total

Test 30: Mixed

Which one letter can be added to the front of all these words to make new words?

Example: ___are ___at ___rate ___all _c_

1 ___less ___east ___rake ___anger ___
2 ___ash ___rite ___inter ___ailing ___
3 ___park ___tripe ___have ___liver ___
4 ___latter ___ink ___ray ___ending ___

Fill in the crosswords so that all the given words are included. You have been given one letter as a clue in each crossword.

5–8

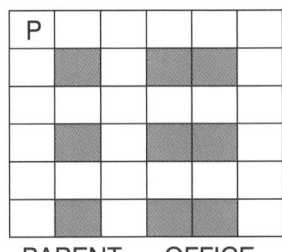
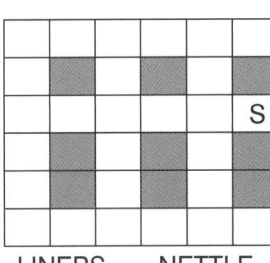
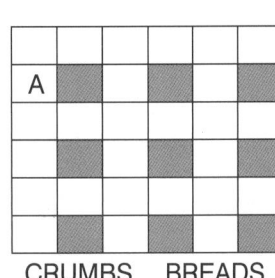
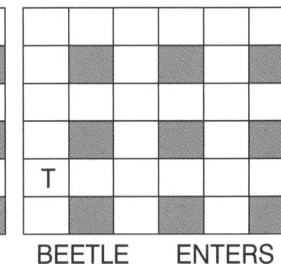

PARENT   OFFICE   LINERS   NETTLE   CRUMBS   BREADS   BEETLE   ENTERS
LANCER   REFINE   ELDEST   DRAINS   USEFUL   POUNDS   TRADER   EXTRAS
POODLE   THEIRS   TEASED   NODULE   NEEDED   CANOPY   BREATH   LARDER

A B C D E F G H I J K L M N O P Q R S T U V W X Y Z

Give the missing letters and numbers in the following sequences. The alphabet has been written out to help you.

Example: CQ   DQ   EP   FP   _GO_   _HO_

9   ___   5W   7Y   ___   7C   5E
10 Ab   Cc   Ed   Ge   ___   ___
11 WCE VEF ___ ___ SKI RMJ
12 PW   ___ TY   VZ   ___ ZB
13 LOC MOE ___ ___ MPK NPM
14 DW   ___ FU   GT   HS   ___

If A = 4, B = 9, E = 2, D = 6, R = 5 and S = 1, find the sum of the following words by adding their letters together.

15 DRESS ___   18 SEEDS ___
16 BREED ___   19 READS ___
17 BEARD ___   20 ADDER ___

Test 31: Mixed

Underline the two words, one from each group, which are the most opposite in meaning.

Example: (dawn, <u>early</u>, wake)   (<u>late</u>, stop, sunrise)

1. (<u>summit</u>, climb, success)   (<u>base</u>, top, ascent)
2. (<u>torrent</u>, river, waterfall)   (<u>trickle</u>, stream, flow)
3. (truly, quietly, thoughtfully)   (truthfully, absolutely, falsely)
4. (sink, <u>robust</u>, dive)   (submerge, swim, <u>sickly</u>)

Underline the two words, one from each group, which are closest in meaning.

Example: (race, shop, <u>start</u>)   (finish, <u>begin</u>, end)

5. (<u>peculiar</u>, subnormal, exact)   (<u>odd</u>, normal, ordinary)
6. (message, note, <u>unseen</u>)   (book, observe, <u>buried</u>)
7. (<u>thrifty</u>, few, elegant)   (numerous, extravagant, <u>frugal</u>)
8. (<u>perch</u>, fly, uphold)   (climb, <u>sit</u>, slide)
9. (effort, take, <u>swivel</u>)   (opportunity, <u>turn</u>, go)

A B C D E F G H I J K L M N O P Q R S T U V W X Y Z

10. If the code for SPEECH is TQFFDI, what is UBMLT? _____
11. If the code for PACKET is RCEMGV, what is ECTFU? _____
12. If the code for BOUGHT is ZMSEFR, what is AJYGK? _____
13. If the code for AROUND is CTQWPF, what is FKBBA? _____
14. If the code for SMILED is VLLKHC, what is KZSOB? _____

The next Thursday after:

15. Thursday 26th March is _____
16. Thursday 3rd April is _____
17. Friday 29th May is _____
18. Saturday 30th June is _____

Read the first two statements. From the information, underline one of the options below that must be true.

19. Gill knocked on her friend's front door. No one answered so she went home.
    A Gill's friend was not home.
    B Gill's friend did not hear her knocking.
    C Gill was unable to visit her friend.
    D Gill's friend was unable to come to the door.

20. My garden has large trees. My garden has flowers which smell lovely when in bloom.
    A My garden doesn't have any grass.
    B My garden has more trees than flowers.
    C My garden has scented flowers.
    D My garden has trees under which flowers are planted.

TEST 32: **Mixed**

Test time: 0 — 5 — 10 minutes

Rearrange the muddled letters in capitals to make a proper word. The answer will complete the sentence sensibly.

Example: A BEZAR is an animal with stripes.   ZEBRA

1 NARAJYU is two months before March.   _____
2 The Titanic sank after hitting an BERCGEI.   _____
3 The dairy farmer milks his herd CITEW a day.   _____
4 The football match NEDDE in a draw.   _____
5 Would you like cheese and SCUBIITS or pudding?   _____

Underline the word in the brackets closest in meaning to the word in capitals.

Example: UNHAPPY (unkind death laughter sad friendly)

6 ENRAGE   (enrich   relax   madden   soothe   calm)
7 DETRACTOR   (digger   critic   supporter builder   follower)
8 APPRECIATE   (neglect cost   value   approach depreciate)
9 MUFFLE   (stifle   scarf   unwrap   sound   ruffle)
10 HINGE   (hanger   door   opening   gateway   joint)

Change the first word into the last word, by changing one letter at a time and making two new different words in the middle.

Example: TEAK   TEAT   TENT   RENT

11 WASH   _____   _____   FIST
12 GRID   _____   _____   DROP
13 GULP   _____   _____   GAOL
14 PINK   _____   _____   BANE

Give the two missing numbers in the following sequences.

Example: 2 4 6 **8** **10**

15 16   15   ___   11   10   ___   7   3
16 14   13   11   ___   ___   7   5   4
17 2   3   ___   8   ___   17   23   30
18 9   10   ___   13   15   ___
19 ___ 15   19   ___   27   31
20 2   ___ 8   16   ___   64

33

Test 33: Mixed

Test time: 0 — 5 — 10 minutes

Sharon's birthday is on 16th January. Mia's birthday is a week before Sharon's. Sara's birthday is two weeks after Sharon's.

1–2 What date is: Mia's birthday? _____   Sara's birthday? _____

Mrs. May was born in 1959 and had a son, Tim, when she was 29.

3–4 How old was: Tim in 1999? _____   Mrs. May in 2007? _____

5 How old will Mrs. May be when her son is 21? _____

A train leaves the local station at 07:30 and the journey to town takes 58 minutes.

6 At what time should the train arrive in town? _____

7 If the train is 17 minutes late, what time does it arrive in town? _____

Fill in the crosswords so that all the given words are included. You have been given one letter as a clue in each crossword.

8–11

WINTER	WILLOW	IMAGES	EMERGE	KITTEN	TANNER	SCHEME	REDEEM
WOODEN	LATEST	SENSES	ESSAYS	BASKET	BATTER	STORMS	TEMPER
TIERED	RETURN	EXISTS	ROGUES	RUNNER	TARTAN	RIOTER	SMOOTH

A B C D E F G H I J K L M N O P Q R S T U V W X Y Z

12 If the code for KINDER is $ 8 a @ ^ ?, what is the code for DINER? _____

13 If the code for AWAKEN is b x b l f o, what is the code for STOP? _____

14 If the code for SPRING is / > ~ ! ^ #, what is the code for GRIPS? _____

15 If the code for TRADER is a n u r s n, what is the code for TREAD? _____

16 If the code for SPONGE is % £ $ # ~ >, what is the code for GONGS? _____

Find two letters which will end the first word and start the second word. The same letters must be used for both pairs of words.

Example: rea (*ch*) air   tou (*ch*) oose

17 biscu (____) em   pla (____) alic   **19** sho (____) ter   ro (____) most

18 flu (____) ipping   wi (____) ower   **20** str (____) pear   he (____) ple

TEST 34: **Mixed**

Test time: 0 5 10 minutes

Find a word that is similar to the word in capital letters and that rhymes with the second word.

Example: CABLE   tyre   ___wire___

1 NERVOUS   fence   _____
2 ARRANGE   sticks   _____
3 SEASHORE   boast   _____
4 STRANGE   beard   _____
5 REMAIN   neigh   _____

Complete the following sentence in the best way by choosing one word from each set of brackets.

Example: Tall is to (tree, <u>short</u>, colour) as narrow is to (thin, white, <u>wide</u>).

6 Path is to (lane, gravel, way) as road is to (tarmac, cars, lines).
7 Stationary is to (paper, still, train) as movement is to (music, active, actor).
8 Near is to (last, next, distant) as close is to (shut, far, local).
9 Race is to (run, compete, win) as is to battle is to (fight, pursue, chase).

A B C D E F G H I J K L M N O P Q R S T U V W X Y Z

Fill in the missing letters. The alphabet has been written out to help you.

Example: AB is to CD as PQ is to RS

10 PN is to LJ as WU is to ____
11 BE is to FG as MP is to ____
12 BA is to ZY as AZ is to ____
13 HI is to GJ as LM is to ____
14 QT is to QN as WZ is to ____
15 GT is to FU as LO is to ____

Change the first word of the third pair in the same way as the other pairs to give a new word.

Example: bind, hind   bare, hare   but, ___hut___

16 patch, pitch   hatch, hitch   watch, _____
17 site, tie   word, rod   silt, _____
18 repatriate, tape   penalty, lane   cenotaph, _____
19 meaningful, meal   hinged, hind   chariot, _____
20 limestone, one   monkey, key   smother, _____

TEST 35: **Mixed**

Test time: 0 – 5 – 10 minutes

Add one letter to the word in capital letters to make a new word. The meaning of the new word is given in the clue.

Example: PLAN simple ___PLAIN___

1 RAIL   feeble   _____
2 PLATED   folded   _____
3 COUCH   bend   _____
4 RIDE   self-worth   _____

Find the four-letter word hidden at the end of one word and the beginning of the next word. The order of the letters may not be changed.

Example: The children had bats and balls.   ___sand___

5 She was so distraught, she dared not go in.   _____
6 Mr Patel drives home and parks the car in the garage.   _____
7 Those boys can be terribly annoying.   _____
8 All of us should succeed given time.   _____
9 The wind blew the newspaper across the park.   _____

A B C D E F G H I J K L M N O P Q R S T U V W X Y Z

10 If the code for NAPKIN is LBNLGO, what is RBZMC?   _____
11 If the code for TWELVE is RUCJTC, what is QCTCL?   _____
12 If the code for BATTLE is DZVSND, what is HHIGV?   _____
13 If the code for PEBBLE is SDEAOD, what is the code for BEACH?   _____
14 If the code for BUTTON is CVUUPO, what is the code for HOLES?   _____
15 If the code for BURDEN is DWTFGP, what is the code for CARRY?   _____

Underline the pair of words most similar in meaning.

Example: come, go   roam, wander   fear, fare

16 despair, destroy   succeed, fail   flourish, thrive
17 death, heaven   life, existence   dead, alive
18 blank, clear   empty, full   vacant, engaged
19 noisy, silent   candid, frank   vocal, vivid
20 front, side   half, whole   signal, gesture

36

Test 36: Mixed

Underline the two words, one from each group, which are the most opposite in meaning.

Example: (dawn, <u>early</u>, wake)   (<u>late</u>, stop, sunrise)

1 (start, finish, leap)   (jump, conclude, walk)
2 (remorse, recur, question)   (reply, repent, repeat)
3 (beneath, over, beside)   (near, inside, under)
4 (slanted, upright, tilted)   (reclined, moving, rushing)

If $p = 4$, $q = 7$, $r = 11$, $s = 3$ and $t = 12$, find the value of the following calculations.

5 $\dfrac{st}{p} - q$ = ____

6 $\dfrac{q + r + t}{s}$ = ____

7 $q^2 - p^2$ = ____

8 $(4q - 2r) \times s$ = ____

9 $qr - (p + s)$ = ____

Underline the two words, one from each group, which are closest in meaning.

Example: (race, shop, <u>start</u>)   (finish, <u>begin</u>, end)

10 (entire, constant, broken)   (complete, part, weary)
11 (part, top, attach)   (resume, split, pierce)
12 (hillock, mountain, cliff)   (pit, hole, mound)
13 (tree, yap, elephant)   (bark, leaf, trunk)
14 (swamp, fill, battle)   (march, swallow, marsh)

A B C D E F G H I J K L M N O P Q R S T U V W X Y Z

Give the missing letters and numbers in the following sequences. The alphabet has been written out to help you.

Example: CQ   DQ   EP   FP   <u>GO</u>   <u>HO</u>

15 DY   EZ   ____   GB   HC   ____
16 ____   5E   7H   ____   11N   13Q
17 sD   ____   oH   ____   kL   iN
18 HS   ____   ____   KP   LO   MN
19 GP64   UQ32   GR16   US8   ____   ____
20 ____   CJN   ____   ENL   FPK   GRJ

Test 37: Mixed

Underline the pair of words most similar in meaning.

Example: come, go   <u>roam, wander</u>   fear, fare

1	sick, nauseous	enriched, impoverished	second-rate, first-class
2	think, mind	ponder, contemplate	brain, brawn
3	claw, beak	talon, limb	paw, foot
4	oppress, iron	depress, sadden	impress, ignore
5	crime, offence	penalty, kick	guilt, innocence

Look at the first group of three words. The word in the middle has been made from the other two words. Complete the second group of three words in the same way, making a new word in the middle.

Example: PAIN INTO TOOK   ALSO <u>SOON</u> ONLY

6	BITE	TEAM	ARMY	WITH	_____	IONS
7	CAMP	CAME	MESS	STIR	_____	OPEN
8	POND	POUR	URNS	FARM	_____	STOP
9	TORE	TIME	LIMP	PUCE	_____	FACT
10	NODE	DONE	BIND	LIFE	_____	FLAG

Change the first word into the last word, by changing one letter at a time and making two new different words in the middle.

Example: TEAK <u>TEAT</u> <u>TENT</u> RENT

11	FARM	_____	_____	HASP
12	LAZY	_____	_____	LIME
13	DEED	_____	_____	ROAD
14	PEST	_____	_____	MEAN

A B C D E F G H I J K L M N O P Q R S T U V W X Y Z

15 If the code for ZINNIA is BKPPKC, what is the code for POPPY? _____

16 If the code for PLANET is RKCMGS, what is the code for EARTH? _____

17 If the code for STREAM is UTTECM, what is the code for RIVER? _____

18 If the code for BASKET is ZYQICR, what is AYPPW? _____

19 If the code for LITTLE is MJUUMF, what is TNBMM? _____

20 If the code for SWEETS is UVGDVR, what is UTIZT? _____

TEST 38: **Mixed**

Test time: 0 5 10 minutes

Give the two missing numbers in the following sequences.

Example: 2   4   6   _8_   _10_

1	5	10	___	17	___	20		
2	3	___	___	4	9	6	12	8
3	___	4	6	7	___	10	12	13
4	7	___	13	16	19	___		
5	___	8	16	___	64	128		
6	4	1	4	3	___	___	4	7

Find the four-letter word hidden at the end of one word and the beginning of the next word. The order of the letters may not be changed.

Example: The children had ba<u>ts and</u> balls.   _sand_

7   Marion's dog ate the cake.   _____
8   Members of that tribe are fierce.   _____
9   The bicycle wheel crushed the petals of a flower.   _____
10   My uncle is too large for his chair.   _____
11   His brother ran out of petrol in his car.   _____

Underline the word in the brackets closest in meaning to the word in capitals.

Example: UNHAPPY   (unkind   death   laughter   <u>sad</u>   friendly)

12	APPLAUD	(apply	clap	claim	arrival	constant)
13	PROSPER	(right	fail	view	chance	flourish)
14	SNAPPY	(twisty	chatty	tetchy	steal	smart)
15	HINDER	(behind	front	back	hamper	picnic)
16	HORDE	(crowd	divide	solo	alone	empty)

Find two letters which will end the first word and start the second word. The same letters must be used for both pairs of words.

Example: rea (_ch_) air   tou (_ch_) oose

17	ro	(___)	ast	tri	(___)	ater
18	bur	(___)	oop	wri	(___)	ump
19	cam	(___)	der	whe	(___)	ves
20	si	(___)	ome	rei	(___)	aw

Total

Test 39: Mixed

Change the first word of the third pair in the same way as the other pairs to give a new word.

Example: bind, hind   bare, hare   but, __hut__

1. dear, deer   pear, peer   read, _____
2. lamp, map   pond, nod   went, _____
3. current, rent   curate, rate   cufflink, _____
4. limpid, dip   organ, nag   mentor, _____
5. biscuit, bit   analogy, any   television, _____

Complete the following sentence in the best way by choosing one word from each set of brackets.

Example: Tall is to (tree, <u>short</u>, colour) as narrow is to (thin, white, <u>wide</u>).

6. Rural is to (country, road, boundary) as urban is to (avenue, crowd, city).
7. Pore is to (spot, flow, skin) as cavity is to (hole, sore, tooth).
8. Bristle is to (brush, hedgehog, thistle) as tooth is to (fang, mouth, comb).
9. Gauge is to (inspect, estimate, purchase) as draft is to (military, outline, complete).

A B C D E F G H I J K L M N O P Q R S T U V W X Y Z

Using the code Z stands for A, Y for B, X for C and so on, decode these words:

10. YZXP _____
11. PMVV _____
12. QVIP _____

Encode these words:

13. HALF _____
14. WORD _____
15. YAWN _____

Underline the word in the brackets which is most opposite in meaning to the word in capitals.

Example: WIDE   (broad   vague   long   <u>narrow</u>   motorway)

16. TIMID   (nervous   shy   bashful   bold   meek)
17. IDIOTIC   (sensible   senseless   careless   thoughtless   edible)
18. SIMPLE   (comprehensible   plain   complex   complete   right)
19. SOLE   (laces   fish   body   single   many)
20. TIMELESS   (late   ageless   enduring   classic   fleeting)

Test 40: Mixed

Add one letter to the word in capital letters to make a new word. The meaning of the new word is given in the clue.

Example: PLAN   simple   ___PLAIN___

1 PLANT celestial body _____
2 CASTE fortified building _____
3 EACH seashore _____
4 LATTER compliment _____

Find the four-letter word which can be added to the letters in capitals to make a new word. The new word will complete the sentence sensibly.

Example: At the zoo, we visited the REP house.   ___TILE___

5 Take the COM with you when you go hiking. _____
6 It is IMANT to take care crossing a road. _____
7 A half added to a half makes one W. _____
8 The queen looked SPID in her ceremonial robes. _____
9 He was filled with DES when he saw the damage to his home. _____

A B C D E F G H I J K L M N O P Q R S T U V W X Y Z

10 If the code for STRIPE is VSUHSD, what is the code for CANDY? _____
11 If the code for DINNER is BGLLCP, what is the code for LUNCH? _____
12 If the code for CASTLE is BBQVIH, what is the code for ARENA? _____
13 If the code for AFRICA is CHTKEC, what is BGDTC? _____
14 If the code for NINETY is LJLFRZ, what is ZFYOQ? _____
15 If the code for RABBIT is PYZZGR, what is FSRAF? _____

There are five trees at the bottom of my garden. Work out where each tree is planted.

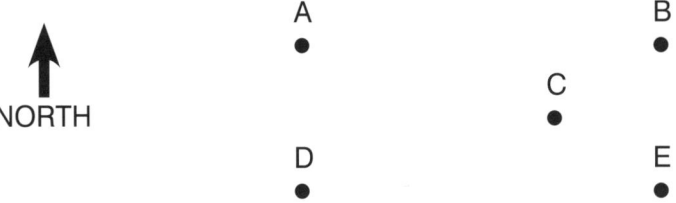

The maple is more northerly than the sycamore but more southerly than the beech. The ash and the oak are west of the sycamore. The oak is northwest of the maple.

16 A _____   19 D _____
17 B _____   20 E _____
18 C _____

Puzzle 1

City Search

Take one letter from the first word and place it in the second word so that two new words are formed. The order of the letters may not be changed. The first word has been done to help you.

Then, rearrange the letters you have removed to make a well-known city and write it on the line. A clue has been provided to help you.

pile	sea	_pie_	_seal_	L
share	beats			
really	wrath			
pine	grim			
shrewd	read			

CITY: _____ A Yorkshire university town.

snore	wide			
mouse	fund			
wander	wet			
drink	rip			
camel	east			
boat	vary			

CITY: _____ A capital choice.

bleak	sack			
rain	sad			
boar	pen			
wring	pay			
meant	rust			
bred	tale			
spear	flight			

CITY: _____ A city in the west of England on the River Avon.

Puzzle 2

Start at the top of the pile of bricks and, working through the layers, make new words by combining two words, one from one layer and the other from the layer below it.

You must go down each time, not sideways.

Here is an example:

Both BLACKOUT and BLACKBERRY are new words, but only OUTDOOR makes sense as the next word.

Now try these. Be careful, there is only one path through!

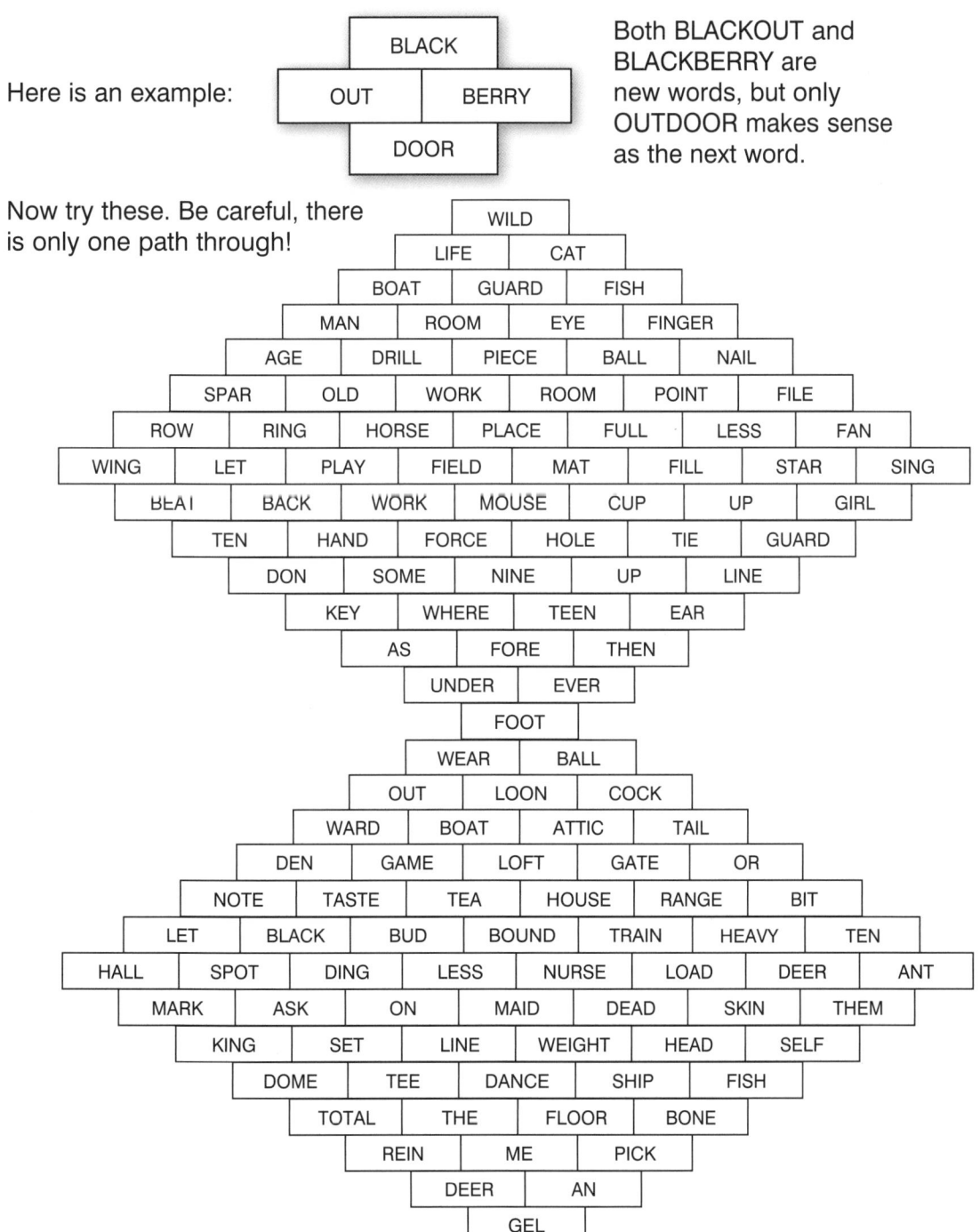

Puzzle 3

Black Jack's Treasure

Here is a pirate's treasure map that is written partly in a letter code and partly in a picture code.

Work out what the information says, then place an X on the spot where the treasure is buried. The alphabet has been written out to help you.

A B C D E F G H I J K L M N O P Q R S T U V W X Y Z

Puzzle 4

Five Square Crossword

Put the words below into the crossword.

EAGER	EARTH	ENROL	ENTER	EPOCH
ERROR	FLAME	FUDGE	GRINS	GROWS
LITHE	LOGIC	RANGE	RIFLE	ROGUE
SORRY	SUNNY	TONIC	TOWEL	TOAST

Puzzle 5

Sunday Activities

Five ladies living in Surrey had good reason for wanting the weather to be fine the following Sunday.

From the information below and using the grid to help you, work out where each lady is going, what they are doing and who they are visiting.

Miss Millard is organising a tennis tournament.

One of the ladies has a niece who lives in Guildford.

The grandchildren are having Sunday lunch in Surbiton.

Mrs Prout and her husband are not going out for a meal.

The countryside near Redhill is where the nature ramble is being planned.

Mrs Snape is visiting her friend's home in Richmond.

Miss Jones does not have grandchildren but she is going out to tea with her niece.

LADY	EVENT	RELATIONSHIP	PLACE
Miss Millard			
Miss Jones			
Mrs Pringle			
Mrs Prout			
Mrs Snape			

Progress Grid

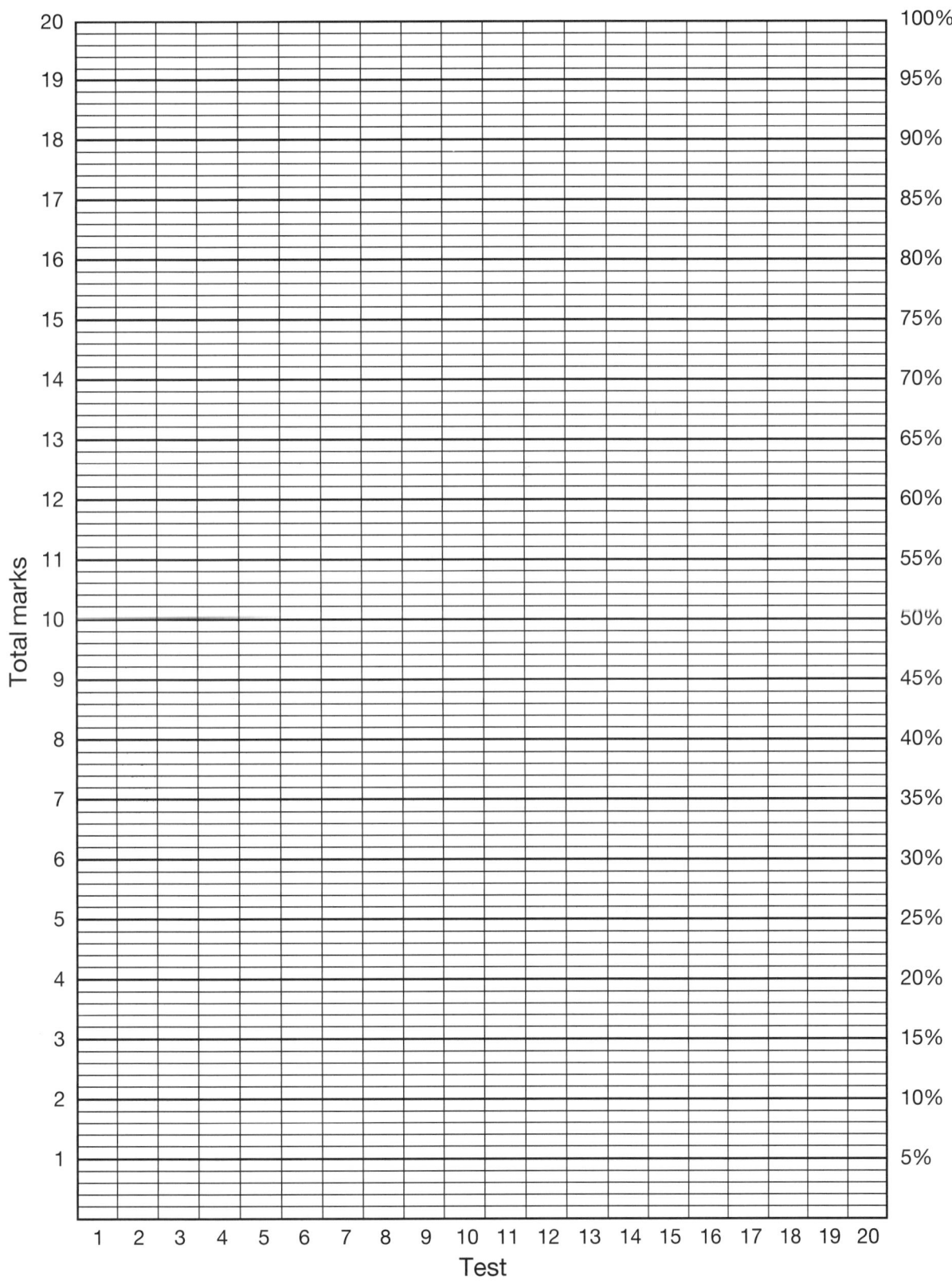

Progress Grid

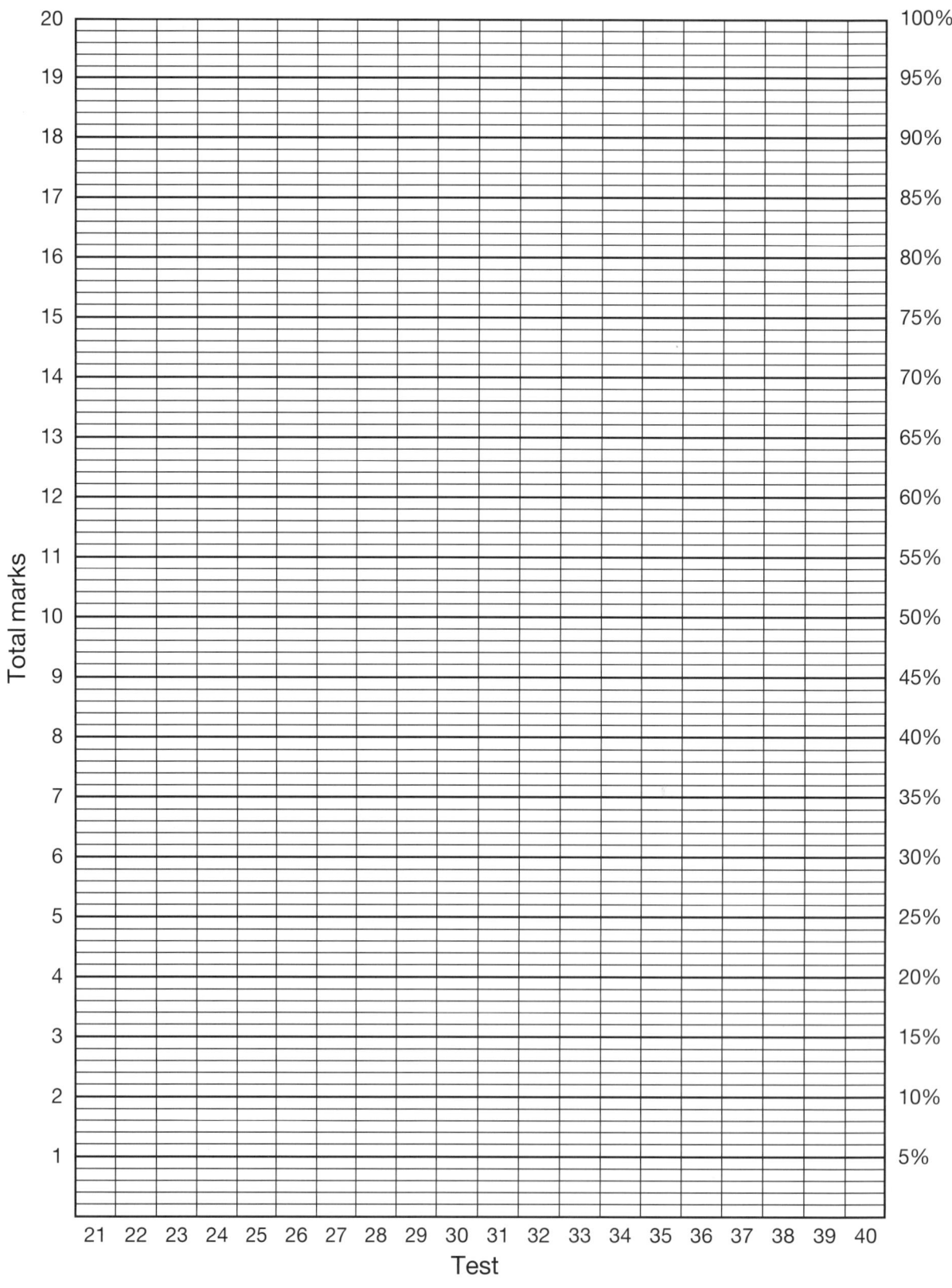